That You Might Believe

DEVOTIONS
ON THE
GOSPEL OF JOHN
FOR TEENS

Book 4

That You Might Believe

ABBY VAN SOLKEMA

REFORMED
FREE PUBLISHING
ASSOCIATION
Jenison, Michigan

Scripture cited is taken from the King James (Authorized) Version

Reformed Free Publishing
1894 Georgetown Center Drive
Jenison, MI 49428
www.rfpa.org
mail@rfpa.org

Cover design by Erika Kiel
Interior design by Katherine Lloyd / theDESKonline.com

ISBN: 978-1-959515-50-0
Ebook ISBN: 978-1-959515-51-7
LCCN: 2025932474

To my husband—thank you for
walking beside me through life's uncertainties
and always pointing me toward our true hope.

INTRODUCTION

In today's world, we often feel as if everything is shifting beneath our feet. The headlines are filled with news of uncertainty—economic struggles, political unrest, natural disasters. Social media presents a constant stream of opinions and pressures, making it hard to find solid ground. It can be difficult to navigate this chaotic world, especially when the future seems uncertain and scary. How can you stay hopeful and grounded when everything around you feels so unpredictable?

The disciples of Jesus also found themselves in a frightening and confusing time as they followed him through the final days of his earthly ministry. In John 16–21, we see them wrestling with fear, confusion, and uncertainty. Jesus had been talking about leaving them, his arrest was imminent, and the reality of his death was sinking in. The disciples were scared, lost, and unsure of what was coming next. The future seemed uncertain, and they didn't fully understand what Jesus had been teaching them about his resurrection and the coming of the Holy Spirit.

In these chapters, Jesus, knowing his disciples' struggles, continues to give words of comfort and encouragement. He assures them that although he will be leaving them physically, he is not abandoning them. His promises about the coming of the Holy Spirit, peace beyond understanding, and the certainty of his victory over death provide the disciples—and each of us—with deep comfort. Jesus' words are not just meant to reassure us in moments of fear but to strengthen our faith in what is to come. He promises that no matter how uncertain the world may feel, he is always with us.

The truth found in the gospel of John is not just an ancient story; it is a timeless message that speaks directly to believers today. In a world filled with doubt and confusion, John's account of Jesus' life, death, and resurrection gives truth that we can hold on to. The exhortation to believe in Jesus and his message is as relevant now as it was for the disciples. As you read these chapters, remember that the comfort and assurance Jesus gave his followers then is also meant for you today. Believing in the truth of God's word is the only way to have both true peace in the midst of life's uncertainties and guidance when you are feeling overwhelmed.

The structure of each day will be as follows: you will first read a passage from John, noting especially the bold-faced verse or verses. Then you will be guided to think about what the passage means by reading the meditation. The "Ask Yourself" section will assist you in applying the truth of Scripture to your life. And finally, the "Praying to Your Heavenly Father" section lists three prayer prompts based on this passage that you can use as a starting point for your own prayer. The journaling space can be used to record your thoughts on the application questions and to write out your prayer.

This volume and the other three in this series are not a comprehensive commentary on the gospel according to John. Rather, they are meant to be a guide to systematically lead you through an entire book of the Bible while familiarizing you with the process of personal Bible study. If you have any questions about the verses that you are reading, I encourage you to talk about them with your parents and siblings, discuss them with godly friends, or go to an elder or pastor for help.

These things have I spoken unto you, that ye should not be offended.

They shall put you out of the synagogues: yea, the time cometh, that whosoever killeth you will think that he doeth God service.

And these things will they do unto you, because they have not known the Father, nor me.

But these things have I told you, that when the time shall come, ye may remember that I told you of them.

DAY 1 – **WARNING OF PERSECUTION**

As Jesus continued giving his disciples their final instructions in the upper room, he warned them about the persecution that they should expect. Not only would the world hate them, but even their own people, the Jews, would turn against them. To be put out of the synagogue (v. 2) is similar to being excommunicated from a church. It meant social rejection by the Jewish community.

Jesus also warned that they may even be killed for confessing that they believed in Jesus. When the false church has political power, as it did in Jesus' day, those who were labeled as heretics could even be persecuted physically. This has happened to many believers over the ages who died at the hands of wicked men—wicked men who think they are serving the church just as the apostle Paul did before he was converted.

Jesus warned his disciples about this persecution for two reasons. The first is that they would not be "offended" (v. 1). The meaning of this word is to stumble and fall. Jesus knew that experiencing the physical and relational effects of persecution is difficult. Can you imagine being forced to leave your church? Family members and friends cutting off contact with you? Even fearing for your life? Would you stay strong? Or would you be tempted to despair or question the truth of God's goodness?

The second reason Jesus gave his disciples this warning was so that they would remember what he said after he was gone and be comforted (v. 4). Christians should expect to be persecuted. As the end of the world draws nearer, this persecution will grow more and more intense. We must prepare for this reality. But Jesus' warning from 2,000 years ago reminds us that even persecution is part of God's perfect plan.

ASK YOURSELF...

Has persecution or pressure from other people ever led you to sin?

. . . .

. . . .

. . . .

. . . .

PRAYING TO YOUR HEAVENLY FATHER

- *Praise* God for his sovereign control over all things.
- *Confess* your own weakness and sinfulness.
- *Ask* him to strengthen your faith so that you can endure persecution.

. . . .

. . . .

. . . .

. . . .

. . . .

. . . .

. . . .

. . . .

. . . .

. . . .

. . . .

And these things I said not unto you at the beginning, because I was with you.

But now I go my way to him that sent me; and none of you asketh me, Whither goest thou?

But because I have said these things unto you, sorrow hath filled your heart.

Nevertheless I tell you the truth; It is expedient for you that I go away: for if I go not away, the Comforter will not come unto you; but if I depart, I will send him unto you.

DAY 2 – **FOR YOUR GOOD**

Jesus's ministry was quickly coming to an end. He was preparing his disciples for his departure and the coming of the Holy Spirit. But the disciples were feeling confused and sad. They didn't fully understand what Jesus was saying about leaving, and they were worried about the future without him as well as the persecution that they would face after he was gone.

However, Jesus assures them that his departure is "expedient" (v. 7), or profitable for them. He was going to prepare a place for them in heaven! The Holy Spirit, who could not be poured out until Jesus left the earth, would be an even better gift than his physical presence. His Spirit would be their constant companion, guide, and comforter. He would teach them, convict them of sin, and lead them into a deeper understanding of God's truth.

But the disciples liked things the way they were now when Jesus was with them in person. They did not understand why Jesus had to die on the cross. Consumed with worry and confusion about the future, they were not even interested in learning more about why and where Jesus was going. His departure, although difficult, was for their benefit, yet their own selfishness kept them from seeking the truth.

Do you or a loved one have health issues? Are you experiencing conflict with family or friends? Are you struggling at school or work? Have these trials ever kept you from seeing the good that God is doing in your life? Jesus' word to his disciples here as he prepared to suffer and die on the cross comes to you as well. Can you imagine if the disciples had gotten what they wanted? Jesus would never have died on the cross to save us from our sins! Our heavenly Father always knows what is best for us even when it is not what we think should happen.

ASK YOURSELF...

Do you trust in God's plan for your life? Or do you become frustrated and bitter when your own plans are delayed or broken?

....

....

....

....

PRAYING TO YOUR HEAVENLY FATHER

- *Thank* God for ordaining a perfect plan for your life.
- Have you doubted God's will for you? *Confess* this sin.
- *Ask* for a desire for spiritual benefits instead of earthly comforts.

....

....

....

....

....

....

....

....

....

....

....

And when he is come, he will reprove the world of sin, and of righteousness, and of judgment:

Of sin, because they believe not on me;

Of righteousness, because I go to my Father, and ye see me no more;

Of judgment, because the prince of this world is judged.

DAY 3 – **THE SPIRIT'S REPROOF**

When the Holy Spirit came, he would work in both the church and the world. One of the primary tasks of the Holy Spirit in the world is to judge and condemn sinful men. The word that is translated in verse 8 as *reprove* is a legal term that means to condemn or convince someone of his or her guilt.

This reproof of the Spirit happens by means of the preaching of the gospel. Lord's Day 31 of the Heidelberg Catechism tells us that the preaching of the gospel is a double-edged sword. It not only opens the kingdom of heaven to believers but also shuts it to unbelievers. By the power of the Spirit, the truth of the gospel message works salvation in the heart of the elect by faith. When this same message is heard by one who does not repent and believe, it leaves that person without excuse and subject to God's righteous judgment.

True preaching of the gospel must contain the three elements that Jesus mentions here: sin, righteousness, and judgment. This message is not a popular one in the world today because most people deny the concept of sin. The world believes that mankind is basically good—no matter how the individual person chooses to live—and thus the world has no reason to fear God or future judgment. Naturally then, they harden their hearts against the message of the gospel.

In contrast to these lies, true preaching shows our complete inability to do what is right, the only standard of righteousness that is explained in God's word, and the certainty of judgment unless we repent and believe. This is the message that we need to hear over and over again, week after week for the rest of our lives, even if we don't always like to hear it—the message that a faithful pastor must bring to his congregation every week. The Spirit uses this preaching to work new life in the hearts of those who believe.

ASK YOURSELF…

What effect does the preaching of the gospel have on your heart and life?

PRAYING TO YOUR HEAVENLY FATHER

- *Praise* God for his perfect righteousness.
- *Ask* for the Spirit's guidance to pinpoint areas of your life where you need to repent of sin.
- Do you have a close friend or family member walking in sin? *Pray* for his or her repentance.

I have yet many things to say unto you, but ye cannot bear them now.

Howbeit when he, the Spirit of truth, is come, he will guide you into all truth: for he shall not speak of himself; but whatsoever he shall hear, that shall he speak: and he will shew you things to come.

DAY 4 – **THE SPIRIT, OUR GUIDE**

As Jesus was bringing this final message to his disciples to a close, he informed them that there was a lot more to learn, but they were not ready to hear it yet (v. 12). He promised that they would continue to learn through the Holy Spirit after he was gone. Jesus said the Spirit of truth would guide them into understanding "all truth" (v. 13).

The Holy Spirit, like a guide, would show them the way to understand God's truth. He would help the apostles understand the meaning of what was about to happen: Jesus' death, resurrection, and return to heaven. The Spirit would help them understand how the Old Testament talked about these key moments and that the kingdom of heaven is spiritual, not earthly.

The Spirit inspired men to write the Old and New Testament books of the Bible, which contain the truth. After the apostles established the New Testament church, the Holy Spirit continued to be a guide for believers throughout the ages. The understanding of doctrine has been developed over the history of the church, recorded in creeds and confessions from which we may learn. The Spirit continues to work in the church today as well.

Jesus' promise here also comes to you: the Holy Spirit will guide you and help you understand the truth. Your understanding of the Bible is not dependent on your own brain power, but on the work of the Spirit in your heart. As you continue to read and learn more about God's word, the Holy Spirit will open your eyes to its deeper meaning and help you apply it to your life. You don't have to understand it all at once, and none of us will ever understand it fully in this life. But you can trust that he is guiding you every step of the way.

ASK YOURSELF...

Have you ever been discouraged or confused in your study of the Bible? How does this passage encourage you?

....

....

....

....

PRAYING TO YOUR HEAVENLY FATHER

- *Praise* God for his faithfulness to his church through many generations.
- *Ask* him to help you better understand his word.
- *Thank* him for the gift of the Holy Spirit's guidance.

....

....

....

....

....

....

....

....

....

....

....

He shall glorify me: for he shall receive of mine, and shall shew it unto you.

All things that the Father hath are mine: therefore said I, that he shall take of mine, and shall shew it unto you.

DAY 5 – **GLORIFY HIM**

The Holy Spirit's mission is not to glorify himself but to glorify the Son. This is central to the doctrine of the Trinity. While the Father, Son, and Holy Spirit are distinct persons, they are one in being, and each member of the Trinity has a unique role. The Holy Spirit does not speak or act independently; instead, he works to reveal the Son, pointing us to him and making him known to us.

The Holy Spirit's role is to take what belongs to Jesus—the truth of who he is, what he does, and the riches of his glory—and declare these to us. The Spirit makes the gospel known, illuminates Scripture, and transforms our hearts to worship Christ. This means that when we hear about the beauty of Christ's work—his perfect life, sacrificial death, and triumphant resurrection—it's the Holy Spirit who works faith in our hearts to believe these things.

Jesus also mentions that "all things that the Father hath are mine" (v. 15), indicating that the relationship between the Father and the Son is one of perfect unity. The Holy Spirit, being sent by both the Father and the Son, works in complete harmony with this divine unity, making known all that is given to the Son, which ultimately leads us to glorify Christ.

The Spirit will prompt you to follow Jesus, whether that's in standing firm in your faith, showing kindness to a friend, or turning away from sin. However, remember that the Holy Spirit will *never* lead you to do something that goes against God's word. He will always guide you according to Scripture. Your role is to listen to his voice as you hear it in the Bible and the preaching and respond in obedience. Trust that as you follow his guidance, you are being conformed more to the image of Christ and bringing glory to his name.

ASK YOURSELF…

How can you more actively listen to the Holy Spirit's guidance in your daily life?

. . . .
. . . .
. . . .
. . . .

PRAYING TO YOUR HEAVENLY FATHER

- *Praise* God for his glory.
- Have you been ignoring the Spirit's guidance in your life? *Confess* this sin.
- *Ask* him to give you the strength to stand firm in the truth.

. . . .
. . . .
. . . .
. . . .
. . . .
. . . .
. . . .
. . . .
. . . .
. . . .

A little while, and ye shall not see me: and again, a little while, and ye shall see me, because I go to the Father.

Then said some of his disciples among themselves, What is this that he saith unto us, A little while, and ye shall not see me: and again, a little while, and ye shall see me: and, Because I go to the Father?

They said therefore, What is this that he saith, A little while? we cannot tell what he saith.

Now Jesus knew that they were desirous to ask him, and said unto them, Do ye enquire among yourselves of that I said, A little while, and ye shall not see me: and again, a little while, and ye shall see me?

Verily, verily, I say unto you, That ye shall weep and lament, but the world shall rejoice: and ye shall be sorrowful, but your sorrow shall be turned into joy.

A woman when she is in travail hath sorrow, because her hour is come: but as soon as she is delivered of the child, she remembereth no more the anguish, for joy that a man is born into the world.

And ye now therefore have sorrow: but I will see you again, and your heart shall rejoice, and your joy no man taketh from you.

And in that day ye shall ask me nothing. Verily, verily, I say unto you, Whatsoever ye shall ask the Father in my name, he will give it you.

Hitherto have ye asked nothing in my name: ask, and ye shall receive, that your joy may be full.

DAY 6 – **SORROW TURNED TO JOY**

As Jesus prepared to leave his disciples, he compared the grief that they would experience after his death to the pain a woman experiences in labor. It would be intense and difficult, but it would result in the overwhelming joy of new life. And Jesus assured his disciples that although they would experience sorrow for a "little while," this sorrow would eventually turn into a joy that no one could take from them.

What did Jesus mean by "your sorrow shall be turned into joy" (v. 20)? The disciples would experience sorrow as they would witness Jesus' death, suffering their own feelings of abandonment and fear. However, when Jesus would rise from the dead, their sorrow would be transformed into joy. Not only that, but the joy that they would experience was not based on circumstances. It was rooted in the resurrection and the relationship they had with Christ. This is the joy that the world cannot take away.

When you feel sorrow or grief, remember that the joy of which Jesus speaks is not dependent on your circumstances. This joy is a gift from God, based on the reality of Jesus' victory over sin and death. Your sorrow may last for a moment, but God's promise of joy in Christ lasts forever. The joy that comes from knowing Jesus is a joy that no one, and nothing, can take away from you.

Jesus also encourages his disciples (and us) to pray with confidence in Jesus' name, knowing that the Father will hear and answer you. This privilege of prayer, made possible through Jesus' sacrificial death and resurrection, enables God's children to receive what they ask in faith, further filling their hearts with joy. As you pray to God in the name of Jesus, remember that the greatest joy you can experience is knowing him more deeply and trusting in his perfect plan for your life.

ASK YOURSELF…

What are some areas in your life where you're experiencing sorrow or difficulty right now?

. . . .
. . . .
. . . .
. . . .

How can you remind yourself of the joy that comes from knowing Jesus, even in the midst of those challenges?

. . . .
. . . .
. . . .
. . . .

PRAYING TO YOUR HEAVENLY FATHER

- *Thank* God for the joy that comes through Jesus' death and resurrection.
- Have you been seeking joy in earthly things? *Confess* this sin.
- *Ask* him to help you remember this joy even in times of sorrow.

These things have I spoken unto you in proverbs: but the time cometh, when I shall no more speak unto you in proverbs, but I shall shew you plainly of the Father.

At that day ye shall ask in my name: and I say not unto you, that I will pray the Father for you:

For the Father himself loveth you, because ye have loved me, and have believed that I came out from God.

I came forth from the Father, and am come into the world: again, I leave the world, and go to the Father.

DAY 7 – **PLAIN SPEECH**

J ust hours before his arrest, Jesus continued to reveal truth that would comfort and strengthen his disciples, not just then, but also for generations to come. He acknowledged that he had been speaking in "proverbs"—parables, analogies, and symbolic language that his disciples sometimes found hard to understand. However, he assured them that a time is coming when he will no longer speak in such obscured ways but will make things plain. This plain speech is the clear revelation of God's will through the gospel, which will be fully realized after Jesus' resurrection and by the power of the Holy Spirit.

In the Old Testament, the priests served as mediators between God and his people. But in the New Testament, the disciples (and all believers) have direct, personal access to the Father through Jesus' name, not because of their own goodness, but because the Father himself loves them. Their love for Jesus and their belief in him as the Son of God are the fruit of his grace. God delights in his children when they love and believe in him.

Finally, in verse 28, Jesus tied everything together by stating how the disciples would gain this clearer revelation and greater access to the Father. Jesus' return to the Father would complete the work of his divine mission. His ascension would show that their salvation is secured and that God's love is the foundation of it all.

Jesus promises that the truths of God, though once hidden in mystery, are now made clear through his life, death, and resurrection. For us, as believers, the gospel is not a puzzle to figure out on our own but a clear declaration that God loves us and has saved us in Christ. This means you don't need to try to "earn" God's love for yourself by figuring out how you need to live so that he accepts you. Instead, you can rest in the simple, clear truth that salvation is in Jesus, and you can approach God directly through him.

ASK YOURSELF…

What comfort do you find in the simplicity of the gospel?

. . . .
. . . .
. . . .
. . . .

PRAYING TO YOUR HEAVENLY FATHER

- *Praise* God for his love.
- *Thank* him for making a way for you to approach him directly.
- *Ask* him to show you ways that you can share the simple message of the gospel with others.

. . . .
. . . .
. . . .
. . . .
. . . .
. . . .
. . . .
. . . .
. . . .
. . . .
. . . .

His disciples said unto him, Lo, now speakest thou plainly, and speakest no proverb.

Now are we sure that thou knowest all things, and needest not that any man should ask thee: by this we believe that thou camest forth from God.

Jesus answered them, Do ye now believe?

Behold, the hour cometh, yea, is now come, that ye shall be scattered, every man to his own, and shall leave me alone: and yet I am not alone, because the Father is with me.

These things I have spoken unto you, that in me ye might have peace. In the world ye shall have tribulation: but be of good cheer; I have overcome the world.

DAY 8 – **HE HAS OVERCOME**

The disciples' reaction in verse 29 revealed not only their excitement but also their misunderstanding. They thought they had figured it all out: Jesus was speaking clearly, and they were confident in their belief. But Jesus, knowing their hearts, recognized that their faith was not as strong as they believed. They were still not prepared for the trials that were coming.

However, Jesus challenged their premature confidence. He questioned their belief, knowing that the time was coming when their faith would be tested. He told them that they would soon be scattered, abandoning him in his hour of need. Despite this, Jesus declared that he was not alone, for the Father would be with him.

But in the face of the disciples' wavering faith, Jesus provided an unshakable hope: "I have overcome the world." This victory was not won in a moment of triumph or by avoiding suffering. Rather, Jesus overcame the world by his obedience to the Father, even unto death on the cross. He defeated sin, death, and the powers of darkness that hold the world in bondage. Through his victory, we have peace. No matter what happens, we can be confident that Christ will have the final victory and our place with him in heaven is secure.

This world threatens to overcome us every minute of our lives. We face insults, struggles, pain, and even death. All of these things could easily steal the joy that is ours in Christ. But Jesus reminds us here that he has already overcome all these things. This is why Paul confesses in Romans 8:37, "In all these things we are more than conquerors through him that loved us." We do not have the power to overcome this world. But he already did it for us. No matter how difficult things get, Jesus' victory is the foundation of our peace.

ASK YOURSELF...

How can you live with the assurance that Jesus has already overcome the world, even when life is hard?

. . . .

. . . .

. . . .

. . . .

What are some ways you can encourage others who are facing tribulations?

. . . .

. . . .

. . . .

. . . .

PRAYING TO YOUR HEAVENLY FATHER

- *Thank* God for his constant presence with you.
- *Ask* him to help you trust in his strength and not your own.
- Do you know someone who is suffering? *Pray* for him or her.

. . . .

. . . .

. . . .

. . . .

. . . .

. . . .

. . . .

. . . .

. . . .

. . . .

These words spake Jesus, and lifted up his eyes to heaven, and said, Father, the hour is come; glorify thy Son, that thy Son also may glorify thee:

As thou hast given him power over all flesh, that he should give eternal life to as many as thou hast given him.

And this is life eternal, that they might know thee the only true God, and Jesus Christ, whom thou hast sent.

I have glorified thee on the earth: I have finished the work which thou gavest me to do.

And now, O Father, glorify thou me with thine own self with the glory which I had with thee before the world was.

DAY 9 – **A PRAYER FOR GLORY**

I n John 17, we find Jesus praying to his Father, right before his arrest and crucifixion. This prayer, known as the high priestly prayer, is one of the most intimate moments recorded in Scripture between Jesus and God the Father. Jesus begins by saying, "The hour is come" (v. 1). This "hour" to which he's referring is his death, which he knows will ultimately bring glory to God and to himself.

In these verses, Jesus reveals a powerful truth about who he is. First, he speaks about his relationship with the Father. He states that he has been given authority over all people to grant eternal life to those who believe in him. Eternal life isn't just about life after death—it's about knowing and loving God for eternity. Jesus came to earth so that we can have this relationship with the Father.

Jesus also speaks about the glory he shared with the Father before the world began. This is another reminder that Jesus is eternal—he existed before time and creation as the triune God. He set aside his eternal glory to come to earth and be humbled. His time on earth is part of an eternal plan to reveal God's glory and give us salvation.

You are at a time in your life when you are figuring out your identity, what really matters, and who you want to be. In a world where it's easy to focus on things like popularity or success, Jesus gives us something far greater—knowing him and experiencing eternal life. His prayer shows us that true glory isn't in our achievements, but in knowing and honoring God. When you live to bring glory to God, whether at school, in friendships, or in your personal goals, you are fulfilling the purpose for which you were created.

ASK YOURSELF...

How can you focus more on bringing glory to God in your daily life, rather than seeking glory in things like school achievements, attention on social media, or popularity?

....

....

....

....

PRAYING TO YOUR HEAVENLY FATHER

- *Praise* God for his eternality.
- *Thank* him for sending his Son so that you may have eternal life.
- *Ask* him to show you how you can honor him in your daily life.

....

....

....

....

....

....

....

....

....

....

....

I have manifested thy name unto the men which thou gavest me out of the world: thine they were, and thou gavest them me; and they have kept thy word.

Now they have known that all things whatsoever thou hast given me are of thee.

For I have given unto them the words which thou gavest me; and they have received them, and have known surely that I came out from thee, and they have believed that thou didst send me.

I pray for them: I pray not for the world, but for them which thou hast given me; for they are thine.

And all mine are thine, and thine are mine; and I am glorified in them.

And now I am no more in the world, but these are in the world, and I come to thee. Holy Father, keep through thine own name those whom thou hast given me, that they may be one, as we are.

While I was with them in the world, I kept them in thy name: those that thou gavest me I have kept, and none of them is lost, but the son of perdition; that the scripture might be fulfilled.

And now come I to thee; and these things I speak in the world, that they might have my joy fulfilled in themselves.

I have given them thy word; and the world hath hated them, because they are not of the world, even as I am not of the world.

I pray not that thou shouldest take them out of the world, but that thou shouldest keep them from the evil.

They are not of the world, even as I am not of the world.

Sanctify them through thy truth: thy word is truth.

As thou hast sent me into the world, even so have I also sent them into the world.

And for their sakes I sanctify myself, that they also might be sanctified through the truth.

DAY 10 – **CHOSEN AND PRESERVED**

As Jesus continued his prayer, we find a beautiful moment where he prayed for his disciples before his crucifixion. In verses 6–9, he asked the Father to protect them, to help them stay faithful, and to make them holy. Jesus knew the challenges his disciples would face in the world, but he was also confident that God would strengthen and guide them through it all.

First, Jesus acknowledged that the disciples belonged to God. He says, "Thine they were, and thou gavest them me" (v. 6). Jesus knew his disciples had been chosen for a special purpose— to continue his mission after he was gone. They were called and set apart by God.

Jesus then prayed for their protection. He asked God to "keep them from the evil [one]" (v. 15). The world they would face was full of temptation and hardship, and Jesus knew that without God's protection, they would struggle. Jesus was essentially asking God to guard their hearts and minds so that they could stay true to him, even when they faced difficulties.

Another important part of Jesus' prayer was his request for the disciples' holiness. He said, "Sanctify them through thy truth: thy word is truth" (v. 17). Knowledge of the truth was vital for the disciples to preach the gospel to the world. And the Spirit uses our increasing knowledge of the truth to more and more transform us into the image of Christ.

It can be easy to feel overwhelmed by the pressures of school, friendships, and the constant noise of the world. But just as Jesus prayed for his disciples, he intercedes with the Father for you, too (Rom. 8:34). Therefore, you can be confident that the power of God will keep you and preserve you all through this life and into eternity (1 Pet. 1:3–5).

ASK YOURSELF...

Where do you turn when you are overwhelmed? To God and his word? Or to earthly things?

....
....
....
....

PRAYING TO YOUR HEAVENLY FATHER

- *Praise* God for his faithfulness to his chosen people.
- *Thank* him for preserving you in this evil world by his power.
- *Ask* him to help you to stay close to God's word and be transformed by it daily.

....
....
....
....
....
....
....
....
....
....
....

Neither pray I for these alone, but for them also which shall believe on me through their word;

That they all may be one; as thou, Father, art in me, and I in thee, that they also may be one in us: that the world may believe that thou hast sent me.

And the glory which thou gavest me I have given them; that they may be one, even as we are one:

I in them, and thou in me, that they may be made perfect in one; and that the world may know that thou hast sent me, and hast loved them, as thou hast loved me.

Father, I will that they also, whom thou hast given me, be with me where I am; that they may behold my glory, which thou hast given me: for thou lovedst me before the foundation of the world.

DAY 11 – **UNITY AND GLORY**

In the third part of Jesus' prayer, we hear him pray for something remarkable—unity and eternal glory for those who will come to believe in him. This prayer was made during Jesus' final hours before his crucifixion. He wasn't just praying for his disciples, but for all believers, including you and me, even though he knew we wouldn't be born for thousands of years.

Jesus prayed "for them also which shall believe on me through their word" (v. 20). This shows how deeply Jesus cares about his people, not just the ones he knew in body on earth, but throughout all of history. He was asking God the Father to protect us and make us one—just as he and the Father are one. The unity for which he prayed is more than just getting along. It's a unity that reflects the relationship he shares with the Father. This is a powerful reminder that our relationships with each other—whether with family, friends, or even classmates—should reflect the same love and unity that Jesus has with God.

But there's more. Jesus also prayed for something even more amazing: eternal glory. He asked that we who believe in him will one day see his glory and be with him forever (v. 24). Jesus was praying that you will experience the fullness of God's love and presence forever. This is the hope that believers have: that one day we will be united with him in heaven, where there is no more pain, sadness, or separation.

You might face challenges that make unity seem difficult, maybe disagreements with friends or feeling misunderstood by others. But remember, Jesus' prayer shows that unity is worth striving for. When you seek to live in peace with others, you're showing the love and unity that all believers have in him.

ASK YOURSELF...

How can you promote unity with your fellow believers?

....

....

....

....

PRAYING TO YOUR HEAVENLY FATHER

- Have you been causing disunity among your family or friends? *Confess* this sin.

- *Thank* God for the love and care he shows you every day.

- *Ask* him to strengthen your faith as you look forward to the peace of heaven.

....

....

....

....

....

....

....

....

....

....

....

O righteous Father, the world hath not known thee: but I have known thee, and these have known that thou hast sent me.

And I have declared unto them thy name, and will declare it: that the love wherewith thou hast loved me may be in them, and I in them.

DAY 12 – **CHRIST IN US**

These final verses in John 17 contain Jesus' plea that his people would know and experience God's deep love and be united with him, reflecting the relationship between the Father and the Son.

First, Jesus spoke about how the world does not know God. He was referring to those still in their sin, separated from God. To know God is not just intellectual, it's relational—knowing him personally and experientially. For believers, this knowledge is made possible through Christ, who reveals the Father. He is the Word made flesh, showing us who God is.

Jesus also spoke of the Father's love for him. This love is not ordinary, human love. It is a perfect, eternal love that has existed within the Godhead before time. Jesus prayed that this very love would be in his people. This means that through Christ we experience the same deep abiding love that the Father has for the Son.

Finally, Jesus mentioned that he would be in his people. This speaks to the believer's union with Christ, a crucial yet difficult doctrine. Through the Holy Spirit, we are united with Christ— his life is our life, his death is our death, his resurrection is our resurrection. And his relationship with the Father is now ours. When Jesus says, "I in them," he is highlighting the close and transformative union that believers share with him.

Our increasingly individualistic culture often leaves people feeling disconnected. But as a child of God, you know the Creator of the universe—not distantly, but intimately through Christ. The more you dive into God's word, spend time in prayer, and cultivate a relationship with him, the more you will experience the knowledge of God that transforms your life.

ASK YOURSELF...

How does the reality of your union with Christ change the way you face challenges in your daily life?

. . . .

. . . .

. . . .

. . . .

PRAYING TO YOUR HEAVENLY FATHER

- *Thank* God for the gift of knowing him through Jesus Christ.
- Have you been neglecting your personal relationship with him? *Confess* this sin.
- *Ask* him to help you live each day with the knowledge of this union.

. . . .

. . . .

. . . .

. . . .

. . . .

. . . .

. . . .

. . . .

. . . .

. . . .

. . . .

When Jesus had spoken these words, he went
forth with his disciples over the brook Cedron,
where was a garden, into the which he entered,
and his disciples.

And Judas also, which betrayed him, knew the
place: for Jesus ofttimes resorted thither with
his disciples.

Judas then, having received a band of men and
officers from the chief priests and Pharisees,
cometh thither with lanterns and torches and
weapons.

Jesus therefore, knowing all things that should
come upon him, went forth, and said unto them,
Whom seek ye?

They answered him, Jesus of Nazareth. Jesus
saith unto them, I am he. And Judas also,
which betrayed him, stood with them.

As soon then as he had said unto them, I am he,
they went backward, and fell to the ground.

Then asked he them again, Whom seek ye? And
they said, Jesus of Nazareth.

Jesus answered, I have told you that I am he: if
therefore ye seek me, let these go their way:

That the saying might be fulfilled, which he
spake, Of them which thou gavest me have I lost
none.

Then Simon Peter having a sword drew it, and smote the high priest's servant, and cut off his right ear. The servant's name was Malchus.

Then said Jesus unto Peter, Put up thy sword into the sheath: the cup which my Father hath given me, shall I not drink it?

DAY 13 – **STANDING STRONG IN FAITH**

John does not record Jesus' sorrowful prayer in the garden of Gethsemane like the other gospel accounts do. In John 18:1–11, we fast forward to the moment when Jesus was arrested. But it is interesting to note that Jesus did not try to hide. He went to a place where he went often, where Judas and the band of men could easily find him.

Jesus was approached by a group of soldiers and religious leaders. Judas betrayed him by leading them to Jesus with a kiss. When the soldiers tried to seize Jesus, Peter, filled with fear and anger, drew his sword and cut off the ear of a servant named Malchus. Jesus responded not with anger, but with calm authority. He told Peter to put away his sword, explaining that this must happen as part of God's plan. Jesus healed Malchus' ear and willingly submitted to being arrested.

This passage shows us a powerful moment of surrender by the Son of God. Jesus knew the suffering that awaited him, yet he didn't resist because he understood that this was the path to fulfill God's plan for salvation. His calmness and obedience contrasted with Peter's impulsive reaction. Peter, trying to protect Jesus, acted out of fear, but Jesus knew that real strength is found in trusting in the Father's timing, even in moments of difficulty.

Jesus' actions here serve as a reminder that following him doesn't always look like standing up for ourselves or reacting in anger when things aren't going our way. It's about trusting God's bigger plan, even when we don't understand it. In your daily life, you might face moments when you feel betrayed, misunderstood, or tempted to act out of frustration. Like Jesus, we are called to remain calm and trust that God is in control. When we respond with patience, even in tough situations, we reflect the strength and peace that only Jesus can give.

ASK YOURSELF...

When faced with difficult situations, do you tend to react impulsively? How can you respond with more patience and faith in your daily life?

. . . .
. . . .
. . . .
. . . .

PRAYING TO YOUR HEAVENLY FATHER

- *Ask* God to help you find peace in his will, especially when it's hard to understand.

- Have you reacted sinfully to a situation out of fear or anger? *Confess* this sin.

- *Praise* him for his perfect control of all things.

. . . .
. . . .
. . . .
. . . .
. . . .
. . . .
. . . .
. . . .
. . . .
. . . .
. . . .

Then the band and the captain and officers of the Jews took Jesus, and bound him,

And led him away to Annas first; for he was father in law to Caiaphas, which was the high priest that same year.

Now Caiaphas was he, which gave counsel to the Jews, that it was expedient that one man should die for the people.

The high priest then asked Jesus of his disciples, and of his doctrine.

Jesus answered him, I spake openly to the world; I ever taught in the synagogue, and in the temple, whither the Jews always resort; and in secret have I said nothing.

Why askest thou me? ask them which heard me, what I have said unto them: behold, they know what I said.

And when he had thus spoken, one of the officers which stood by struck Jesus with the palm of his hand, saying, Answerest thou the high priest so?

Jesus answered him, If I have spoken evil, bear witness of the evil: but if well, why smitest thou me?

Now Annas had sent him bound unto Caiaphas the high priest.

DAY 14 – **STANDING STRONG IN TRUTH**

In these two passages from John 18, we read about the beginning of Jesus' trial, where he was questioned by Annas, the former high priest, and Caiaphas, the current high priest. Annas had been the high priest for many years before the Romans removed him, but he still held significant influence. Caiaphas, his son-in-law, was the current high priest and the one who would ultimately play a key role in the decision to crucify Jesus.

As Jesus was questioned by Annas, he remained calm and confident. Annas wanted to know about Jesus' teachings and his disciples. Jesus responded in a straightforward way in verse 20, saying that his ministry was public, and all the Jews had plenty of opportunity to hear his teaching. Jesus' words remind us that he has always been open and honest. He didn't hide anything from anyone, and his message was clear to all who would listen.

When Jesus was struck by one of the officers for answering boldly, he didn't retaliate. Instead, he responded calmly again. He asked them in verse 23 to point out what he had said that was wrong, but if they couldn't, why were they punishing him? Jesus stood firm in the truth, even when faced with injustice. He fulfilled the prophecy of Isaiah 53 of a servant who would suffer unjustly for the sins of his people.

At times in your life, you will face pressure to hide your beliefs, keep quiet about what's right, or go along with what's popular. But Jesus' example calls us to stand strong in the truth, even when it's difficult. We are to speak the truth with love and confidence, not because it's always easy, but because it honors God. In a world that often values acceptance over truth, we are called to be like Jesus—standing firm, speaking openly, and trusting that God is with us every step of the way.

ASK YOURSELF...

How can you stand strong in your faith and speak the truth with love when you face pressure to remain silent or compromise your beliefs?

. . . .

. . . .

. . . .

. . . .

PRAYING TO YOUR HEAVENLY FATHER

- *Praise* God for his truth.
- Have you kept silent when you should have stood up for the truth? *Confess* this sin.
- *Ask* God to give you the courage to stand firm in your faith and to speak the truth boldly, even when it's hard or uncomfortable.

. . . .

. . . .

. . . .

. . . .

. . . .

. . . .

. . . .

. . . .

. . . .

. . . .

. . . .

JOHN 18:28-40

Then led they Jesus from Caiaphas unto the hall of judgment: and it was early; and they themselves went not into the judgment hall, lest they should be defiled; but that they might eat the passover.

Pilate then went out unto them, and said, What accusation bring ye against this man?

They answered and said unto him, If he were not a malefactor, we would not have delivered him up unto thee.

Then said Pilate unto them, Take ye him, and judge him according to your law. The Jews therefore said unto him, It is not lawful for us to put any man to death:

That the saying of Jesus might be fulfilled, which he spake, signifying what death he should die.

Then Pilate entered into the judgment hall again, and called Jesus, and said unto him, Art thou the King of the Jews?

Jesus answered him, Sayest thou this thing of thyself, or did others tell it thee of me?

Pilate answered, Am I a Jew? Thine own nation and the chief priests have delivered thee unto me: what hast thou done?

Jesus answered, My kingdom is not of this world: if my kingdom were of this world, then

would my servants fight, that I should not be delivered to the Jews: but now is my kingdom not from hence.

Pilate therefore said unto him, Art thou a king then? Jesus answered, Thou sayest that I am a king. To this end was I born, and for this cause came I into the world, that I should bear witness unto the truth. Every one that is of the truth heareth my voice.

Pilate saith unto him, What is truth? And when he had said this, he went out again unto the Jews, and saith unto them, I find in him no fault at all.

But ye have a custom, that I should release unto you one at the passover: will ye therefore that I release unto you the King of the Jews?

Then cried they all again, saying, Not this man, but Barabbas. Now Barabbas was a robber.

DAY 15 – **NOT OF THIS WORLD**

Next we see Jesus standing before Pontius Pilate, the Roman governor, as he faced accusations from the Jewish leaders. Pilate was a powerful man, known for his role in maintaining order for the Roman Empire. He was the one who had the authority to pass the death sentence, and his question to Jesus, "Art thou the King of the Jews?" (v. 33), set the stage for a crucial moment in Jesus' trial.

Jesus responded, "My kingdom is not of this world" (v. 36), revealing that his rule and reign are not bound to earthly power or politics. Jesus made it clear that he is the king of a spiritual kingdom, one that isn't defined by the systems of this world. His subjects will fight spiritual battles, not physical ones. Pilate, however, struggled to understand this. His perspective was limited to earthly authority, and he couldn't fully grasp the truth that Jesus was revealing.

It's easy to get caught up in the pressures of the world around us—whether it's fitting in at school, dealing with social media, or thinking about our future. Pilate's confusion represents how we often view life based on temporary, worldly standards. But Jesus calls us to look beyond that. He shows us that his kingdom is eternal. It is defined by truth, love, and grace, not by worldly power.

When Jesus says, "Everyone that is of the truth heareth my voice" (v. 37), he reminds us that only his people can believe in and submit to his kingly rule by faith. By faith, we can trust in Jesus and his kingdom, no matter the pressures or confusion we face. We are called to live with our eyes set on eternal truths, finding our identity in him rather than in the fleeting things of this world.

ASK YOURSELF…

In what areas of your life are you tempted to focus on worldly success or approval instead of the truth and values of God's kingdom?

....

....

....

....

How can you shift your perspective in these areas?

....

....

....

....

PRAYING TO YOUR HEAVENLY FATHER

- *Praise* God for his omnipotence, his unlimited power.
- *Thank* him for giving you the gift of faith.
- *Ask* him to help you set your heart on the eternal values of his kingdom rather than on worldly success or the approval of others.

....

....

....

....

....

....

....

....

....

....

JOHN 18:15–18

And Simon Peter followed Jesus, and so did another disciple: that disciple was known unto the high priest, and went in with Jesus into the palace of the high priest.

But Peter stood at the door without. Then went out that other disciple, which was known unto the high priest, and spake unto her that kept the door, and brought in Peter.

Then saith the damsel that kept the door unto Peter, Art not thou also one of this man's disciples? He saith, I am not.

And the servants and officers stood there, who had made a fire of coals; for it was cold: and they warmed themselves: and Peter stood with them, and warmed himself.

JOHN 18:25–27

And Simon Peter stood and warmed himself. They said therefore unto him, Art not thou also one of his disciples? He denied it, and said, I am not.

One of the servants of the high priest, being his kinsman whose ear Peter cut off, saith, Did not I see thee in the garden with him?

Peter then denied again: and immediately the cock crew.

DAY 16 – **PETER'S DENIAL**

In these passages from John 18, we read about a low moment in the life of Peter, one of Jesus' closest disciples. In the face of questioning, Peter denied knowing Jesus three times, to three different people. Just hours before, he had boldly pledged never to abandon Jesus, but in a moment of weakness, his fear won out. But before you are too hard on Peter, remember that we are all capable of failing when we rely on our own strength.

Peter's unfaithfulness contrasts sharply with Jesus' unwavering faithfulness. While Peter faltered, Jesus stayed true to his calling, knowing that he would soon face the cross to take the punishment for all our sins. This contrast reminds us of our own sinful nature—we often fall short, giving in to temptation or fear. But unlike us, Jesus is always faithful, even when we fail.

Peter's story also reveals how God responds to our failures. Jesus knew Peter would deny him, yet Matthew 16:18 tells us that he still chose Peter to lead his church. After the resurrection, Jesus restored Peter with love and forgiveness. This teaches us that no matter how many times we fail, God's grace is always greater than our sin. He will not leave our prayers for forgiveness unanswered.

When we fall into sin, it's easy to feel hopeless or ashamed. But just like Peter, we can find restoration in our faithful Father. His love for us can never be taken away because it is based on the sacrifice of our sinless Savior on the cross, not on our own ability to follow his law. He will hear and answer our prayers for forgiveness and help us fight against sin by the power of his Spirit.

ASK YOURSELF...

How can you trust in his faithfulness rather than your own strength next time you face temptation or fear?

. . . .

. . . .

. . . .

. . . .

PRAYING TO YOUR HEAVENLY FATHER

- *Thank* God for his faithfulness.
- Have you tried to rely on your own strength? *Confess* this sin.
- *Ask* him to remind you of his grace and love when you feel weak.

. . . .

. . . .

. . . .

. . . .

. . . .

. . . .

. . . .

. . . .

. . . .

. . . .

. . . .

Then Pilate therefore took Jesus, and scourged him.

And the soldiers platted a crown of thorns, and put it on his head, and they put on him a purple robe,

And said, Hail, King of the Jews! and they smote him with their hands.

Pilate therefore went forth again, and saith unto them, Behold, I bring him forth to you, that ye may know that I find no fault in him.

Then came Jesus forth, wearing the crown of thorns, and the purple robe. And Pilate saith unto them, Behold the man!

When the chief priests therefore and officers saw him, they cried out, saying, Crucify him, crucify him. Pilate saith unto them, Take ye him, and crucify him: for I find no fault in him.

The Jews answered him, We have a law, and by our law he ought to die, because he made himself the Son of God.

When Pilate therefore heard that saying, he was the more afraid;

And went again into the judgment hall, and saith unto Jesus, Whence art thou? But Jesus gave him no answer.

Then saith Pilate unto him, Speakest thou not unto me? knowest thou not that I have power to crucify thee, and have power to release thee?

Jesus answered, Thou couldest have no power at all against me, except it were given thee from above: therefore he that delivered me unto thee hath the greater sin.

And from thenceforth Pilate sought to release him: but the Jews cried out, saying, If thou let this man go, thou art not Caesar's friend: whosoever maketh himself a king speaketh against Caesar.

When Pilate therefore heard that saying, he brought Jesus forth, and sat down in the judgment seat in a place that is called the Pavement, but in the Hebrew, Gabbatha.

And it was the preparation of the passover, and about the sixth hour: and he saith unto the Jews, Behold your King!

But they cried out, Away with him, away with him, crucify him. Pilate saith unto them, Shall I crucify your King? The chief priests answered, We have no king but Caesar.

Then delivered he him therefore unto them to be crucified.

DAY 17 – **KING OF THE JEWS**

In John 19, we find Jesus standing before the Roman governor, Pontius Pilate, just before his crucifixion. Pilate, who was unsure of what to do with Jesus, presented him to the crowd, saying, "Behold your King!" (v. 14). Pilate was mocking the Jewish leaders, who had accused Jesus of being a king, because Jesus' claim to kingship seemed so absurd to him. Pilate didn't fully understand the gravity of the situation, but he was playing a pivotal role in the fulfillment of God's plan of redemption.

The chief priests, who rejected Jesus as their Messiah, responded by shouting, "We have no king but Caesar" (v. 15). This was a shocking declaration because Israel, God's chosen people, were supposed to acknowledge God as their true king. But at this moment, they were openly rejecting Jesus and aligning themselves with the Roman emperor. The chief priests mocked, scorned, and rejected the one who is the true king of all creation.

Jesus is king, but not in the way the world expects. Pilate and the Jewish leaders failed to understand the nature of Jesus' kingship, even though in his ministry, Jesus repeatedly explained that his kingdom is "not of this world" (John 18:36). His reign is spiritual, not political, and it is centered on the salvation of his people.

The world has its own ideas about what a king looks like: someone who is wealthy, strong, and in control. But Jesus' kingship is different. He is humble, compassionate, and he rules with love and justice. His throne is not a palace, but a cross. And through his death, he conquers sin, death, and the grave. Jesus is the true king, whose reign will never end.

The rejection of Jesus as king by the Jewish leaders here should challenge us to think about our own lives. It's easy to say with our lips that Jesus is king, but do our actions reflect that he truly rules over us? You will face many temptations to live as if you are your own king, pursuing your own desires and following the ways of the world. But true freedom is found in acknowledging Jesus as king.

ASK YOURSELF...

How do you view Jesus as king in your life? Do you recognize his rule in everyday moments?

....

....

....

....

PRAYING TO YOUR HEAVENLY FATHER

- *Praise* God for his sovereign rule over all things.

- Have you been rejecting his lordship in any areas of your life? *Confess* this sin.

- *Ask* him to help you follow the humble, compassionate example of Jesus.

....

....

....

....

....

....

....

....

....

....

....

And they took Jesus, and led him away.

And he bearing his cross went forth into a place called the place of a skull, which is called in the Hebrew Golgotha:

Where they crucified him, and two other with him, on either side one, and Jesus in the midst.

And Pilate wrote a title, and put it on the cross. And the writing was Jesus Of Nazareth The King Of The Jews.

This title then read many of the Jews: for the place where Jesus was crucified was nigh to the city: and it was written in Hebrew, and Greek, and Latin.

Then said the chief priests of the Jews to Pilate, Write not, The King of the Jews; but that he said, I am King of the Jews.

Pilate answered, What I have written I have written.

Then the soldiers, when they had crucified Jesus, took his garments, and made four parts, to every soldier a part; and also his coat: now the coat was without seam, woven from the top throughout.

They said therefore among themselves, Let us not rend it, but cast lots for it, whose it shall be: that the scripture might be fulfilled, which saith, They parted my raiment among them, and for my vesture they did cast lots. These things therefore the soldiers did.

DAY 18 – **A SOVEREIGN PLAN**

In this passage, we witness the brutal reality of Jesus' crucifixion—the climax of his lifelong suffering and humiliation, and ultimately his death. It is easy to focus on the pain and tragedy of the cross, but for the believer, this moment is the culmination of God's sovereign plan for salvation.

As Jesus walked toward Golgotha, bearing the cross, he was not a victim of circumstances. He was the Savior who willingly laid down his life, fulfilling the Father's will (John 10:18). The mocking, the insults, the agony—they were part of the ordained plan of God to redeem his people. This was not a plan that was thrown together by human hands, but a plan that God, in his infinite wisdom and grace, set in motion before the foundation of the world (Ephesians 1:4).

The sign above Jesus' head, "Jesus Of Nazareth, The King Of The Jews," was not merely a declaration of mockery from Pilate, but a statement of divine truth. Jesus is indeed the king of the Jews, and he is the king of all who trust in him. His kingship is not one of earthly power or dominance but of sacrificial love and redemption. In this moment of deepest humiliation, Jesus established his eternal reign.

The crucifixion of Jesus wasn't a random event, nor was it merely a tragedy. It was God's predetermined plan for the redemption of his people. As we read in Acts 2:23, Jesus was "delivered [up] by the determinate counsel and foreknowledge of God." His death was not an accident, but part of God's eternal plan to save a people for himself. We can trust that nothing in our lives happens outside of God's sovereign control. In moments of trial or uncertainty, remember that God's sovereign plan is unfolding in your life. Jesus' death was not an accident, and neither are the struggles you face today. Trust in his sovereign hand.

ASK YOURSELF...

How does remembering that there are no accidents change the way that you view the events of your life?

....

....

....

....

PRAYING TO YOUR HEAVENLY FATHER

- *Praise* God for his love and mercy.
- *Thank* him for sending his Son to die for your sins.
- *Ask* him to help you trust in his sovereignty over all things.

....

....

....

....

....

....

....

....

....

....

....

Now there stood by the cross of Jesus his mother, and his mother's sister, Mary the wife of Cleophas, and Mary Magdalene.

When Jesus therefore saw his mother, and the disciple standing by, whom he loved, he saith unto his mother, Woman, behold thy son!

Then saith he to the disciple, Behold thy mother! And from that hour that disciple took her unto his own home.

After this, Jesus knowing that all things were now accomplished, that the scripture might be fulfilled, saith, I thirst.

Now there was set a vessel full of vinegar: and they filled a spunge with vinegar, and put it upon hyssop, and put it to his mouth.

When Jesus therefore had received the vinegar, he said, It is finished: and he bowed his head, and gave up the ghost.

DAY 19 – IT IS FINISHED

Jesus was crucified in public, surrounded by mockers, soldiers, and loved ones. John, the disciple "whom he loved," stood beside Mary, Jesus' mother. As Jesus hung on the cross, he wasn't suffering only physically; he was also taking on the sins of his people, experiencing God's wrath in our place. Yet, even in his suffering, Jesus showed care for others, entrusting his mother to John. This act revealed Jesus' deep love and concern for his people, even in his darkest hour.

When Jesus declared, "It is finished" (v. 30), he wasn't just acknowledging the end of his life but proclaiming redemption's completion. These words confirm Christ's sacrifice as sufficient. Jesus did not just make salvation possible—he accomplished it. "Finished" means perfectly completed. Jesus' death wasn't merely an example of love but the full atonement for sin, satisfying God's justice.

Nothing more is needed for salvation—no good works, rituals, or efforts can add to what Jesus has done. This is the heart of the gospel: Jesus bore our sin and paid the price completely. It's a finished work, a completed salvation, given freely to all who believe.

You might not always feel as if you're living in the "finished" reality of the cross. Life—homework, friendships, family tensions—can feel overwhelming. In times like these, remember that Jesus' words, "It is finished," are not just for adults. They are for you, right now.

Jesus' death and resurrection mean that you don't need to earn God's love. Your mistakes and failures don't disqualify you from his grace. When you fail, instead of trying to "fix" yourself—run to the cross. Your redemption is secured. Jesus has done all the work. You can rest in his grace.

ASK YOURSELF...

How does knowing that "it is finished" help you with the struggles or sins you face in daily life?

. . . .

. . . .

. . . .

. . . .

PRAYING TO YOUR HEAVENLY FATHER

- *Praise* God for his grace.
- *Thank* him for the work of salvation that was accomplished on the cross.
- *Ask* him to help you rest in the fact that you don't have to earn his love.

. . . .

. . . .

. . . .

. . . .

. . . .

. . . .

. . . .

. . . .

. . . .

. . . .

. . . .

The Jews therefore, because it was the preparation, that the bodies should not remain upon the cross on the sabbath day, (for that sabbath day was an high day,) besought Pilate that their legs might be broken, and that they might be taken away.

Then came the soldiers, and brake the legs of the first, and of the other which was crucified with him.

But when they came to Jesus, and saw that he was dead already, they brake not his legs:

But one of the soldiers with a spear pierced his side, and forthwith came there out blood and water.

And he that saw it bare record, and his record is true: and he knoweth that he saith true, that ye might believe.

For these things were done, that the scripture should be fulfilled, A bone of him shall not be broken.

And again another scripture saith, They shall look on him whom they pierced.

DAY 20 – **BLOOD AND WATER**

The Roman soldiers, to ensure that Jesus was truly dead before the Sabbath began, pierced his side with a spear. As a soldier's spear pierced Jesus' side, blood and water poured out. This wasn't just a random detail added to the story. John, the author of this gospel, intentionally included it to show us something important about who Jesus is and what he accomplished on the cross.

First, we need to remember the significance of the blood and water in the context of Jesus' death. The blood symbolizes his sacrifice for sin. Throughout the Old Testament, blood was associated with atonement. When an animal was sacrificed, its blood was shed as a covering for sin (Lev. 17:11). But Jesus' blood, shed on the cross, is the final and perfect sacrifice. His death removes the penalty of sin permanently for all who trust in him (Heb. 9:12–14).

The water that poured out with the blood symbolizes the cleansing and renewal that Jesus gives through the Holy Spirit. Water often represents purification in the Bible (Ezek. 36:25–27). Jesus' blood cleanses us from sin, but the water reminds us that he also gives us new life by his Spirit. This is made possible only by Jesus' work on the cross.

The blood he shed paid the full price for your sins—past, present, and future. There's nothing more you need to do to earn God's favor, and you don't need to keep feeling guilty or ashamed when you repent and believe and are truly sorry for your sins. The water that flowed out of Jesus' side reminds you that your salvation is also a work of God's Spirit. You are not left alone to figure things out on your own. The Holy Spirit, who gives you new life, works in you every day to help you grow in holiness.

ASK YOURSELF...

Where else do you regularly see the signs of blood and water?

....

....

....

....

How does this deepen your understanding of Jesus' complete sacrifice for your sins and the ongoing work of the Holy Spirit in your life?

....

....

....

....

PRAYING TO YOUR HEAVENLY FATHER

- *Praise* God for his perfect justice.
- *Thank* him for cleansing you from all your sin.
- *Ask* him to help you walk in the power of his Spirit.

....

....

....

....

....

....

....

....

....

....

....

And after this Joseph of Arimathaea, being a disciple of Jesus, but secretly for fear of the Jews, besought Pilate that he might take away the body of Jesus: and Pilate gave him leave. He came therefore, and took the body of Jesus.

And there came also Nicodemus, which at the first came to Jesus by night, and brought a mixture of myrrh and aloes, about an hundred pound weight.

Then took they the body of Jesus, and wound it in linen clothes with the spices, as the manner of the Jews is to bury.

Now in the place where he was crucified there was a garden; and in the garden a new sepulchre, wherein was never man yet laid.

There laid they Jesus therefore because of the Jews' preparation day; for the sepulchre was nigh at hand.

DAY 21 – A PROPER BURIAL

At the end of John 19, we read about two men who, until this moment, had remained largely in the shadows of Jesus' story: Joseph of Arimathea and Nicodemus. Both were members of the Jewish council, the Sanhedrin, and both, fearing the rejection or persecution they might face from their peers, had secretly followed Jesus (John 19:38). Now, after Jesus' death on the cross, they came out of the shadows.

Joseph of Arimathea boldly asked Pilate, the Roman governor, for permission to take Jesus' body. Nicodemus, the man who had once visited Jesus at night to ask questions (John 3:1–2), joined him and brought a generous amount of spices for Jesus' burial. The two men carefully prepared Jesus' body and laid it in a tomb near the place of his crucifixion.

First and foremost, this passage confirms the reality of Jesus' death. As Lord's Day 16 of the Heidelberg Catechism states, "Why was he also buried? Thereby to prove that he was really dead." His burial in a tomb was not symbolic; it was a physical, historical event. Jesus really died. This is crucial because the Bible teaches that "the wages of sin is death" (Rom. 6:23), and Jesus took the punishment for sin upon himself, dying in our place. The physicality of his death is important because it shows that Jesus fully experienced the consequences of sin, even though he himself was sinless.

Without a death, there can be no resurrection. Jesus' body was laid in the tomb, but it wouldn't stay there. In three days, he would rise again, conquering death and securing eternal life for all who believe in him. The resurrection is the foundation of the Christian faith. Without it, Christianity would be meaningless (1 Cor. 15:17). But because of the resurrection, we have hope that death is not the end. When we face our own death or the death of a loved one and fellow believer, we can rejoice even in our sorrow, because we know that all of God's children will be together with him one day, in body and soul.

ASK YOURSELF...

What are some ways you can live out the reality of Jesus' victory over sin and death in your daily life?

. . . .

. . . .

. . . .

. . . .

PRAYING TO YOUR HEAVENLY FATHER

- *Praise* God for his steadfast love.
- *Thank* him for the death and resurrection of Jesus Christ.
- *Ask* him to help you remember that death is not the end.

. . . .

. . . .

. . . .

. . . .

. . . .

. . . .

. . . .

. . . .

. . . .

. . . .

. . . .

JOHN 20:1-18

The first day of the week cometh Mary Magdalene early, when it was yet dark, unto the sepulchre, and seeth the stone taken away from the sepulchre.

Then she runneth, and cometh to Simon Peter, and to the other disciple, whom Jesus loved, and saith unto them, They have taken away the Lord out of the sepulchre, and we know not where they have laid him.

Peter therefore went forth, and that other disciple, and came to the sepulchre.

So they ran both together: and the other disciple did outrun Peter, and came first to the sepulchre.

And he stooping down, and looking in, saw the linen clothes lying; yet went he not in.

Then cometh Simon Peter following him, and went into the sepulchre, and seeth the linen clothes lie,

And the napkin, that was about his head, not lying with the linen clothes, but wrapped together in a place by itself.

Then went in also that other disciple, which came first to the sepulchre, and he saw, and believed.

For as yet they knew not the scripture, that he must rise again from the dead.

Then the disciples went away again unto their own home.

But Mary stood without at the sepulchre weeping: and as she wept, she stooped down, and looked into the sepulchre,

And seeth two angels in white sitting, the one at the head, and the other at the feet, where the body of Jesus had lain.

And they say unto her, Woman, why weepest thou? She saith unto them, Because they have taken away my Lord, and I know not where they have laid him.

And when she had thus said, she turned herself back, and saw Jesus standing, and knew not that it was Jesus.

Jesus saith unto her, Woman, why weepest thou? whom seekest thou? She, supposing him to be the gardener, saith unto him, Sir, if thou have borne him hence, tell me where thou hast laid him, and I will take him away.

Jesus saith unto her, Mary. She turned herself, and saith unto him, Rabboni; which is to say, Master.

Jesus saith unto her, Touch me not; for I am not yet ascended to my Father: but go to my brethren, and say unto them, I ascend unto my Father, and your Father; and to my God, and your God.

Mary Magdalene came and told the disciples that she had seen the Lord, and that he had spoken these things unto her.

DAY 22 – **KNOWN AND LOVED**

The gospel of John records one of the most powerful moments in history: the resurrection of Jesus Christ. In John 20, we read about Mary Magdalene's encounter with the risen Lord. This passage begins with Mary discovering the empty tomb early on the first day of the week, after Jesus' crucifixion. At first, she assumed someone had stolen Jesus' body. She ran to tell Peter and John, and they came to see the tomb for themselves.

But when Mary stayed behind, she saw something more. She encountered two angels in the tomb, who asked her why she was weeping. In her grief and confusion, she turned around and saw someone standing there—Jesus, though she didn't recognize him immediately. Jesus spoke her name, and suddenly she realized that it was the risen Christ. She responded with joy and worship, but Jesus told her not to cling to him, for he had not yet ascended to the Father. Instead, he commissioned her to go tell his disciples that he had risen.

When Jesus called Mary by name, he showed that he knew her personally and loved her. The resurrection was not just a powerful event in the past; it continues to affect each and every believer personally. Jesus calls you by name too. In the midst of your doubts, fears, or failures, Jesus knows you and calls you to follow him.

Jesus didn't leave Mary in her grief but spoke to her personally. Do you ever feel unnoticed or as if no one truly understands you? Your Savior knows you personally (see Psalm 139). His resurrection means he is alive and you are alive in him. His love is constant and enduring. Take comfort in knowing that the King of kings calls you by name.

ASK YOURSELF...

How does remembering that God knows you personally give you comfort in your daily life?

. . . .
. . . .
. . . .
. . . .

PRAYING TO YOUR HEAVENLY FATHER

- *Praise* God for his perfect knowledge of all things— including you.
- *Thank* him for the amazing gift of the resurrection.
- *Ask* him to remind you that he knows you by name.

. . . .
. . . .
. . . .
. . . .
. . . .
. . . .
. . . .
. . . .
. . . .
. . . .
. . . .

Then the same day at evening, being the first day of the week, when the doors were shut where the disciples were assembled for fear of the Jews, came Jesus and stood in the midst, and saith unto them, Peace be unto you.

And when he had so said, he shewed unto them his hands and his side. Then were the disciples glad, when they saw the Lord.

Then said Jesus to them again, Peace be unto you: as my Father hath sent me, even so send I you.

And when he had said this, he breathed on them, and saith unto them, Receive ye the Holy Ghost:

Whose soever sins ye remit, they are remitted unto them; and whose soever sins ye retain, they are retained.

DAY 23 – **SENT AND EQUIPPED**

The events in this passage take place on the evening of the day Jesus rose from the dead. The disciples were hiding in fear behind locked doors, uncertain and scared after Jesus' crucifixion. Imagine the fear and confusion they must have felt—everything they had hoped for seemed to be lost. Then, in a moment that must have been both surprising and overwhelming, Jesus appeared in their midst.

Jesus' greeting, "Peace be unto you," was not just a simple "hello." It was a blessing. After his death, they were living in turmoil, fear, and guilt. Jesus' resurrection brought peace—not just peace in circumstances, but peace with God. Through his death Jesus had made atonement for sin, and now his resurrection proved that the price had been paid. Then Jesus showed them his hands and side—the marks of the crucifixion. This was proof that he was indeed the same Jesus who had died.

But Jesus didn't just bring peace; he also commissioned them. Just as God the Father sent Jesus to proclaim the kingdom and bring salvation, so Jesus sent his followers into the world to continue that work. But he didn't leave them powerless. He breathed on them and gave them the Holy Spirit. The Holy Spirit equips believers to fulfill the mission of God.

Finally, Jesus gave the disciples authority to forgive sins. This doesn't mean that they or we have the power to forgive sins in ourselves, but it points to the gospel message we're called to support. When people hear the good news of Jesus and repent, their sins are forgiven through Christ alone.

Jesus doesn't just save us for our own sake; he calls us to take part in his mission. While not everyone is called to go and preach, we are all called to support those whom God sends. We can pray for missionaries and pastors as they labor to bring the gospel to the world. We can encourage them, provide for their needs, and strengthen the work of the church by faithfully participating in it.

ASK YOURSELF...

How can you support those who are working to spread the gospel?

....
....
....
....

PRAYING TO YOUR HEAVENLY FATHER

- *Thank* God for the peace that you have in Christ.
- Have you been neglecting to support the spread of the gospel? *Confess* this sin.
- *Ask* him to strengthen and equip those who he has called to ministry.

....
....
....
....
....
....
....
....
....
....
....

JOHN 20:24–29

But Thomas, one of the twelve, called Didymus, was not with them when Jesus came.

The other disciples therefore said unto him, We have seen the Lord. But he said unto them, Except I shall see in his hands the print of the nails, and put my finger into the print of the nails, and thrust my hand into his side, I will not believe.

And after eight days again his disciples were within, and Thomas with them: then came Jesus, the doors being shut, and stood in the midst, and said, Peace be unto you.

Then saith he to Thomas, Reach hither thy finger, and behold my hands; and reach hither thy hand, and thrust it into my side: and be not faithless, but believing.

And Thomas answered and said unto him, My Lord and my God.

Jesus saith unto him, Thomas, because thou hast seen me, thou hast believed: blessed are they that have not seen, and yet have believed.

DAY 24 - **DOUBTING THOMAS**

In John 20, Jesus had already risen from the dead and had appeared to his disciples to show them that he was alive. In this particular passage, we meet Thomas, one of the twelve, who wasn't present when Jesus first appeared to the other disciples (John 20:19–23). Because of this absence, Thomas was skeptical when the other disciples told him that Jesus had risen. He demanded physical proof—he wanted to see the nail marks in Jesus' hands and the wound in his side before he would believe. Thomas' doubt here has earned him the nickname "Doubting Thomas" in Christian tradition, but it's important to remember that his response is a very human one. He wanted something tangible to confirm what he had heard.

A week later, Jesus appeared again to his disciples and gave Thomas the very proof he asked for. But Jesus didn't just give Thomas evidence; he called him to stop doubting and believe. Thomas responded with a declaration of faith: "My Lord and my God!" (v. 28). Jesus then spoke a blessing over those who would believe in him without having seen him—a blessing that extends to all believers who trust in Christ through the testimony of Scripture.

The passage highlights the difference between believing through seeing and believing through faith. Jesus blesses those who believe without physical evidence. God calls us to trust him even when we can't see him with our eyes. It's not about the proof we can touch or see, but about trusting in the testimony of Scripture and the Holy Spirit's work in our hearts.

Your faith is a gift from God. The Holy Spirit works in your heart to help you trust in God's word, which is full of the testimony of Jesus' life, death, and resurrection. In moments of doubt or fear, don't be afraid to bring your questions and doubts to God just as Thomas did. He will help you grow in your trust and love for him as you continue to follow him.

ASK YOURSELF...

In moments of doubt or uncertainty, how can you strengthen your trust in God's word and his promises, even when you don't have tangible evidence?

. . . .

. . . .

. . . .

. . . .

PRAYING TO YOUR HEAVENLY FATHER

- *Praise* God for his patience and grace.

- Do you have doubts? *Bring* them to God in prayer.

- *Ask* him to give you the faith to believe in something that you cannot see.

. . . .

. . . .

. . . .

. . . .

. . . .

. . . .

. . . .

. . . .

. . . .

. . . .

And many other signs truly did Jesus in the presence of his disciples, which are not written in this book:

But these are written, that ye might believe that Jesus is the Christ, the Son of God; and that believing ye might have life through his name.

DAY 25 – **THAT YOU MIGHT BELIEVE**

As you have read through the gospel of John, you have learned about the miracles that Jesus performed during his life—miracles that pointed to his true identity as the Son of God. John's gospel is distinct in that it highlights specific signs that demonstrate Jesus' deity and his mission to bring eternal life to all who believe in him.

In these verses, John reflects on his purpose in writing the gospel. John didn't write just to inform us about Jesus' life or to give us interesting stories. While many other things could have been written about Jesus' life, by the inspiration of the Holy Spirit John chose to record specific signs that would lead his readers to the most important conclusion: Jesus is the Christ, the Messiah, the Son of God.

There are so many voices around you—friends, social media, teachers, celebrities—telling you what to believe, what is cool, and what will bring fulfillment. You may also struggle with doubt or wonder if faith in Jesus is worth it. The question with which John leaves us is: Do you believe in Jesus? Not just as a historical figure or a character in a book, but as the Son of God, the one who came to save you from your sins and give you eternal life. And this is not just about intellectual belief. It's about having a spiritual knowledge of God and being confident that he is the only way of salvation.

When John says that by believing in Jesus, we "might have life through his name" (v. 31), he's referring to the new life that comes through faith in Christ. You don't have to wait until you're older to experience the power of God in your life. If you believe, you have the transforming power of the Holy Spirit in your heart. You can experience his peace, his purpose, and his direction in your life right now. And, most importantly, you have assurance that no matter what happens, your future is secure in Jesus.

ASK YOURSELF...

Do you believe that Jesus is the Christ, the Son of God? If so, how does that belief shape the way you live your life today?

....

....

....

....

PRAYING TO YOUR HEAVENLY FATHER

- *Praise* God for revealing himself to you through his word.
- *Thank* him for the gift of eternal life.
- *Ask* him to strengthen your faith.

....

....

....

....

....

....

....

....

....

....

....

After these things Jesus shewed himself again to the disciples at the sea of Tiberias; and on this wise shewed he himself.

There were together Simon Peter, and Thomas called Didymus, and Nathanael of Cana in Galilee, and the sons of Zebedee, and two other of his disciples.

Simon Peter saith unto them, I go a fishing. They say unto him, We also go with thee. They went forth, and entered into a ship immediately; and that night they caught nothing.

But when the morning was now come, Jesus stood on the shore: but the disciples knew not that it was Jesus.

Then Jesus saith unto them, Children, have ye any meat? They answered him, No.

And he said unto them, Cast the net on the right side of the ship, and ye shall find. They cast therefore, and now they were not able to draw it for the multitude of fishes.

Therefore that disciple whom Jesus loved saith unto Peter, It is the Lord. Now when Simon Peter heard that it was the Lord, he girt his fisher's coat unto him, (for he was naked,) and did cast himself into the sea.

And the other disciples came in a little ship; (for they were not far from land, but as it were two hundred cubits,) dragging the net with fishes.

As soon then as they were come to land, they saw a fire of coals there, and fish laid thereon, and bread.

Jesus saith unto them, Bring of the fish which ye have now caught.

Simon Peter went up, and drew the net to land full of great fishes, an hundred and fifty and three: and for all there were so many, yet was not the net broken.

Jesus saith unto them, Come and dine. And none of the disciples durst ask him, Who art thou? knowing that it was the Lord.

Jesus then cometh, and taketh bread, and giveth them, and fish likewise.

This is now the third time that Jesus shewed himself to his disciples, after that he was risen from the dead.

DAY 26 – **COME AND DINE**

The beginning of John 21 records the third time Jesus appeared to his disciples. The disciples were at the Sea of Tiberias (also known as the Sea of Galilee), and they had gone back to what they knew best—fishing. Notice that despite their experience, the disciples caught nothing. They worked hard all night but still had empty nets. Then Jesus appeared on the shore, though they didn't recognize him at first, and he gave them a simple command: "Cast the net on the right side of the ship." When they obeyed, they caught an overwhelming number of fish.

Jesus already had fish cooking on the fire when they landed, and he called them to share a meal with him. This moment highlights the grace and provision of the risen Lord. Jesus met their needs in a tangible way and showed them that he is with them, even in the ordinary things of life.

Jesus provides abundantly for his people, both physically and spiritually. Just as he provided fish for the disciples, he provides everything we need for life and godliness (2 Pet. 1:3). The catch of 153 fish shows the abundance of Christ's grace toward his people. In him, we have more than enough. As Paul confesses in Philippians 4:19, "But my God shall supply all your need according to his riches in glory by Christ Jesus."

Whether you're studying for a test, handling a difficult relationship, or dealing with disappointment, ask your heavenly Father for help. He is sovereign over every part of your life, and he cares about even the smallest details. Relying on your own ability to take care of things will only lead to disappointment. Pray for guidance and trust that he will provide what you need, even when it feels like you're not succeeding on your own.

ASK YOURSELF...

What are some specific ways that God has provided for your needs?

....
....
....
....

PRAYING TO YOUR HEAVENLY FATHER

- *Thank* him for his love and provision.
- Have you been trying to do things in your own strength? *Confess* this sin.
- *Ask* him to help you trust him in all areas of your life.

....
....
....
....
....
....
....
....
....
....
....

So when they had dined, Jesus saith to Simon Peter, Simon, son of Jonas, lovest thou me more than these? He saith unto him, Yea, Lord; thou knowest that I love thee. He saith unto him, Feed my lambs.

He saith to him again the second time, Simon, son of Jonas, lovest thou me? He saith unto him, Yea, Lord; thou knowest that I love thee. He saith unto him, Feed my sheep.

He saith unto him the third time, Simon, son of Jonas, lovest thou me? Peter was grieved because he said unto him the third time, Lovest thou me? And he said unto him, Lord, thou knowest all things; thou knowest that I love thee. Jesus saith unto him, Feed my sheep.

Verily, verily, I say unto thee, When thou wast young, thou girdest thyself, and walkedst whither thou wouldest: but when thou shalt be old, thou shalt stretch forth thy hands, and another shall gird thee, and carry thee whither thou wouldest not.

This spake he, signifying by what death he should glorify God. And when he had spoken this, he saith unto him, Follow me.

DAY 27 – **FEED MY SHEEP**

After Jesus and the disciples had finished their meal of bread and fish, Jesus spoke directly to Peter. He asked him three times, "Lovest thou me?" This repetition was not just about questioning Peter's affection; it also paralleled Peter's three denials. Each time Peter answered, Jesus gave him a command: "Feed my lambs," "feed my sheep," and "feed my sheep" (vv. 15–17).

Jesus was commissioning Peter (and by extension, all believers) to take part in the work of the kingdom of God. Jesus called his disciples to shepherd others, feeding them with his word, just as a shepherd cares for his flock. Lambs and sheep represent the people of God, the church, whom Peter was called to care for spiritually.

The command "feed my sheep" emphasizes the importance of spiritual nourishment. As a shepherd feeds sheep, Peter (and all of us) must ensure that God's people are nurtured with the gospel, the truth of God's word. This is not just about knowledge or teaching—it's about loving and nurturing others in Christ. It involves patient guidance, correction, encouragement, and always pointing others to the grace of God in Jesus Christ.

Jesus also made reference to Peter's future, when he would be martyred for his faith (v. 18). Following Jesus is not always easy, and there is a cost involved. But even with this cost, Jesus' call to "follow me" remains, pointing us to the joy and reward found in faithfully serving God.

You may not be a pastor, but Jesus' command to "feed my sheep" is still relevant. One way we can do this is by praying for our pastors, elders and deacons as they faithfully shepherd God's people. They bear the responsibility of preaching, teaching, and leading the church, often at great personal cost. We can also encourage others to join a church where they will be spiritually fed through the preaching of God's word and the sacraments. Being part of a faithful church community is essential for our growth in Christ.

ASK YOURSELF...

How can you support the officebearers in your church?

. . . .

. . . .

. . . .

. . . .

How can you help others commit to a church where they will receive spiritual nourishment?

. . . .

. . . .

. . . .

. . . .

PRAYING TO YOUR HEAVENLY FATHER

- *Praise* God for his gracious work in your heart and life.
- *Thank* him for the nourishment that he gives you in his word.
- *Ask* him to help you faithfully love others as he has loved you.

. . . .

. . . .

. . . .

. . . .

. . . .

. . . .

. . . .

. . . .

. . . .

. . . .

Then Peter, turning about, seeth the disciple whom Jesus loved following; which also leaned on his breast at supper, and said, Lord, which is he that betrayeth thee?

Peter seeing him saith to Jesus, Lord, and what shall this man do?

Jesus saith unto him, If I will that he tarry till I come, what is that to thee? follow thou me.

Then went this saying abroad among the brethren, that that disciple should not die: yet Jesus said not unto him, He shall not die; but, If I will that he tarry till I come, what is that to thee?

This is the disciple which testifieth of these things, and wrote these things: and we know that his testimony is true.

And there are also many other things which Jesus did, the which, if they should be written every one, I suppose that even the world itself could not contain the books that should be written. Amen.

DAY 28 – **FOLLOW ME**

In this passage, we find Peter, having just been restored by Jesus after denying him three times, asking a question that many of us might want to ask: What about that person? Peter noticed John, the disciple Jesus loved, following them and wanted to know what John's future held. But Jesus' answer was striking: "What is that to thee? Follow thou me" (v. 22).

Jesus had just told Peter that he would die for him and that following Jesus would involve sacrifice (vv. 18–19). So, Peter's question about John was not just curiosity; it was a comparison. He wanted to know if John's path would be easier or harder than his own. Jesus, however, redirected Peter's focus. The call to follow Jesus is a personal one, and it doesn't depend on what others are doing or how God is working in their lives.

This passage reminds us of a key truth: we are not called to follow someone else's path. We are called to follow Jesus. In our own lives, it's easy to compare our walk with others, whether it's someone we know in person or someone we follow on social media. Why does that person seem to have it easier? Why does his path look different from mine? Jesus' response to Peter challenges us: Don't worry about someone else's journey; focus on following Jesus where he has called you.

In your daily life, whether at school, participating in sports, or in your relationships, focus on your personal walk with Jesus. God's plan for your life is unique, and he has called you to follow him, no matter the cost. Let go of comparisons. What is it that Jesus is asking of you today? Are you willing to follow him, even when the way looks different from the way he calls others to follow?

ASK YOURSELF...

In what areas of your life is God calling you to focus more on him and less on the lives of others?

....

....

....

....

PRAYING TO YOUR HEAVENLY FATHER

- *Thank* God for the guidance that he gives in his word. Have you been jealous or envious of others?

- *Confess* this sin.

- *Ask* for strength to persevere in your unique calling as a child of God.

....

....

....

....

....

....

....

....

....

....

....

DEVOTIONS ON
THE GOSPEL OF JOHN FOR TEENS

Read them all!

These four 1-month devotionals follow Jesus' ministry as relayed by the apostle John. Each devotional emphasizes the importance of confessing that Jesus Christ is God and also provides many practical applications for teen readers.

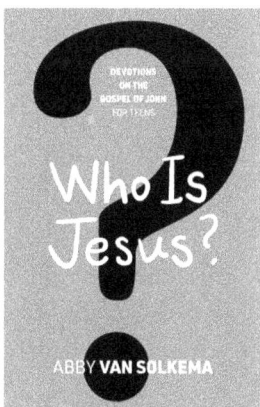

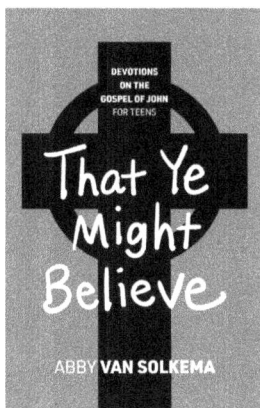

Available at rfpa.org

www.ingramcontent.com/pod-product-compliance
Lightning Source LLC
Chambersburg PA
CBHW072359090426
42741CB00012B/3084